Chariots of Chrome

CLASSIC AMERICAN CARS OF CUBA

Chariots

CLASSIC AMERICAN

The BOSTON
MILLS PRESS

# of Chrome

CARS OF CUBA

SIMON BELL
&
GEORGE FISCHER

A BOSTON MILLS PRESS BOOK

Published by Boston Mills Press, 2004
132 Main Street, Erin, Ontario N0B 1T0
Tel: 519-833-2407 Fax: 519-833-2195
e-mail: books@bostonmillspress.com
www.bostonmillspress.com

In Canada:
Distributed by Firefly Books Ltd.
66 Leek Crescent
Richmond Hill,
Ontario, Canada L4B 1H1

In the United States:
Distributed by Firefly Books (U.S.) Inc.
P.O. Box 1338, Ellicott Station
Buffalo, New York 14205

National Library of Canada Cataloguing in Publication

Fischer, George, 1954-
Chariots of chrome : classic American cars of Cuba /
by George Fischer and Simon Bell.

ISBN 1-55046-394-2

1. Antique and classic cars — Cuba — Pictorial works. 2. Antique and classic cars —
United States — Pictorial works. I. Bell, Simon M. (Simon MacDonald) II. Title.

TL33.C83F47 2004   629.222'097291   C2003-901190-9

Publisher Cataloging-in-Publication Data   (U.S.)

Fischer, George, 1954-
Chariots of chrome : classic American cars of Cuba /
by George Fischer and Simon Bell. 1st ed. [144] p. : col. photos. ;   cm.
Summary: Photographs and essays on the restoration, maintenance and
love of classic American cars in Cuba.

ISBN 1-55046-396-9

1. Antique and classic cars Cuba—Pictorial works. 2. Antique and
classic cars United States — Pictorial works. I. Bell, Simon M. (Simon MacDonald). II. Title.

629.222/ 097291 21   TL33.C83F47 2003

The publisher acknowledges for their financial support of our publishing program,
the Canada Council, the Ontario Arts Council and the Government of Canada
through the Book Publishing Industry Development Program (BPIDP).

Design by Gillian Stead

Printed in Singapore

Colorful colonial buildings line the main street of Matanzas, where it is common to see all kinds of horsepower.

To my father,
Group Captain
James Frank MacDonald Bell, D.F.C.,
a heroic man, generous with his love,
who gave me my first camera at age six.
Frank may well have seen some of the cars
in this book as senior military officer
on a Canadian diplomatic mission
to Havana in February 1953.

I wish to thank all the Cuban people
who helped me complete this project and I
salute their indomitable spirit and unfailing
hospitality in these difficult times.

To Karl Fischer, Pam Fischer,
Kathy and Ervin Gardos, and the
red Mustang, the green Peugeot,
the blue Malibu and all the cars that
gave us great memories from our
childhood (especially the car
I demolished in Trout Lake).

Contents

Introduction

THE WORLD'S LARGEST LIVING MUSEUM OF AMERICAN CARS

Cuba is a vintage car lover's paradise. Until the 1960s Cuba was the world's leading importer of American automobiles. These chariots of chrome were brought from Florida by the boatload, to the great delight of those members of pre-Revolution society who could afford their luxury.

Havana in the 1940s and '50s embraced all things American, incorporating them into Cuba's exotic blend of Spanish and African cultures. Glamorous nightclubs thrived, and Hollywood celebrities were drawn to this intoxicating mix of local style and American affluence. All makes and models of American cars, with their luscious curves and futuristic grills and fins, cruised the streets of the old city.

But the Revolution brought a swift end to upper-class lavishness, and resulting political tensions led to a total embargo on exports from the United States to Cuba. The island nation soon found itself in a kind of vacuum of worldly goods, with each American-made car becoming an irreplaceable object.

It is estimated that as many as ten thousand mid-century American cars still exist in Cuba, making this country perhaps the world's largest living automotive museum. While most North Americans, in their continuing quest for the new, gladly relegate

Parked outside the Hotel Nacional is a rare burgundy 1955 DeSoto Diplomat. This model is in fact a Plymouth body with DeSoto trim and nameplate. Some export model DeSotos were Diplomats, but a true DeSoto expert would notice that the recognizable seven-tooth grille is missing from this version.

A Cuban taxi pulls away from the Capitolio and onto Calle Brasil with its human cargo destined for various parts of the country.

their autos to the scrap pile after a mere ten years' service, generations of inventive Cuban mechanics have lovingly maintained their precious American cars. Some have been restored to their former glory, others have been elaborately improvised into working condition by transplants of Soviet truck engines and hand-forged parts.

Today, vintage Buicks, Cadillacs, Chevys, Dodges, Fords, Hudsons, Pontiacs, Ramblers and Studebakers still spice up the streets of Cuba's cities and its coastal highways with their hot primary colors and dazzlingly ornate chrome, their sinfully expansive interiors and defiantly unmodern girth.

On O'Reilly Street, with the Plaza de la Catedral nearby, two young Cuban boys lean against an antiquated 1950 Dodge Wayfarer. Cuban children often use immobilized cars on the streets as American kids use neighborhood playground equipment.

A silver ghost gleams in the morning light on a narrow street in Old Havana.

The ornate facades of Havana's buildings recall a grander time when the city was the most important seaport in the Caribbean.

A massive wrought-iron portrait of Commandante Che Guevara, based on the iconic photo by Korda, dominates the vast Plaza de la Revolución in central Havana.

The Museum of the Revolution, with its magnificent interior designed by Tiffany, was home to Cuba's presidents prior to 1959. Behind the museum are a number of vehicles that played a role in the revolution. The "Fast Delivery" truck, riddled with bullet holes, was used by the revolutionaries to launch an attack in 1957 on the very building that now houses the museum. All the attackers were killed and Fidel Castro went to jail.

A sporty Mercury convertible, reconditioned and ready to rent — for American dollars only.

A red-and-white Cadillac roars up the Paseo de Martí, also known as the Prado. In its heyday, the Prado resembled the Champs Elysées, with couples strolling the wide boulevard in the shade of the immense trees. The center of the two-way boulevard is an island walkway flanked by ornate gas lamps, benches and bronze lions.

A group of Cuban boys enjoy a rest after a game of soccer in the Plaza de Armas.

Sunset over the white dome of the Capitolio and the ornate Gran Teatro.

Golden rays of light catch the
neoclassical buildings across
from the Parque Central.

Spandex leggings are all the rage among Cuban women, young and old. Colorful clothes and bright smiles reflect the indomitable Cuban spirit.

A horse-drawn carriage transports tourists past the Edificio Bacardí.

Hundreds of Packards, Buicks, Chevys
and Oldsmobiles, both taxi versions
and private cars, roar up the Prado
daily from the Malecón, past the
Parque Central, Inglaterra Hotel and
the Teatro, to park in neat, angled
rows of two in front of the Capitolio.
The *boteros* patiently participate
in "La Cola," Cuban slang
for waiting in line.

Many privately owned cars in Cuba are used as
unofficial taxis called *boteros*. With limited public
transportation available, *boteros* are an indispensable
service for Cubans. Inexpensive but off limits to tourists,
these noisy old American cars are frequently crammed
with up to eight passengers and their baggage, collected
and dropped on predetermined routes.

An early evening view looking down the tree-lined Prado to the sea, where the lighthouse at El Morro castle marks the entrance to Havana Bay.

The former presidential palace, now the Museo de la Revolución, contains everything one would ever want to know about Fidel Castro, Che Guevara and the 1953–59 Cuban Revolution. Parked in the front entrance is a Soviet-made armored tank, aiming skyward as if ready to fire. Coincidentally, parked at the curb directly in front of the tank is a black 1957 Chevy Bel Air, looking somewhat dangerous and militaristic itself.

A siesta in the Plaza Vieja
is the perfect antidote to a
hot Havana afternoon.

The 1954 Chevrolet Bel Air Townsman, "just the ticket for those trips to the wide open spaces" claimed the ads of the day.
This particular vehicle found a long and productive life serving as a taxi.

Work, rest and play, the fabric of daily life unfolds on the streets of Old Havana.

Trafficless streets provide an impromptu venue for the Grand Old Game.

Even without access to proper equipment, Cuban children are passionate about baseball.

Camellos, CoCo Taxis and Peso Taxis

Getting around in Cuba is a problem for most Cubans. Tourists can rent a car or take a tour bus, but most Cubans can't afford that luxury. In the towns, bicycles get many people where they need to go. In the country, travel is still often on horseback.

With few cars and even fewer buses on the roads, hitchhiking is a necessary mode of travel for young and old alike. Government vehicles are obliged to pick up hitchhikers, and trucks are often seen loaded with travelers as their primary cargo.

In Havana, large Russian buses known as "camels," because of their twin-humped shape, are a familiar sight. These buses are usually bursting at the seams with passengers and are sometimes referred to by the locals as *la Pelicula de Sabado* ("Saturday night movie"), as they are said to be filled with sex, violence and bad language.

Whizzing past at irregular intervals are the yellow CoCo taxis, shaped like coconuts, hence the name. They are fast and cheap, but due to their pollution output, passengers are advised to wear gas masks. They belch and wheeze and dodge the bicycle rickshaws and over-passengered motorcycles.

Peso taxis are Frankenstein versions of American cars from the '50s, kept running with parts from Ladas and Russian trucks, tractors and other farm machinery. It's often impossible to correctly distinguish the model, year or even make of these cars. Officially, only Cubans are allowed to ride in these contraptions that cost as little as ten pesos a ride. Because of their poor condition — and because the government runs a fleet of modern taxis — these *boteros*, as they are also known, are off limits to tourists.

A magnificent swan hood ornament seems to mimic this Cuban woman's drooped neck and shoulders.

A green Zephyr on Calle Brasil just outside the Plaza Vieja.

Schoolchildren do their daily exercises on the Paseo del Prado.

On stormy days when waves pound the seawall of the Malecón,
most old cars seek an alternate route to avoid the corrosive saltwater spray.

Cacharros Particular

High on the pecking order of Cuban automobiles are the privately owned, pampered and polished beauties that can be seen parading the streets of Havana and other island cities. These private cars can be identified by their yellow license plates bearing the word Particular.

Many of these cars are meticulously maintained by their owners, though parts must often be cannibalized from identical but more distressed models or crafted by one of the country's necessarily inventive mechanics.

Due to the United States' longstanding embargo against Cuba, very few cacharros sport 100-percent original parts. In most cases, the cars' odometers, like the country itself, have seen more than a couple of revolutions. And while it's a sure bet that the radio won't work, each shiny chrome push-button relic looks as though it's about to blare Jerry Lee Lewis or the Big Bopper from its dashboard speakers.

The best of these private vintage cruisers are proudly displayed at car competitions, and the best of the best are frequently owned by members of exclusive car clubs such as the Automobile Club of Havana.

1960 Chevy Impala

A red 1960 Chevy Impala owned by
Marid Christina Cuesta Ugaete sits
collecting dust from the renovations
going on near the corner of Obispo and
the Plaza de Armas. Named after an
African antelope, this car was defined by
chief engineer Ed Cole as the "prestige
car within reach of the average American
citizen." The Impala became America's
best-selling car 1960.

Alfredo Zalhuar parked his 1957 Buick Roadmaster outside the restaurant where he was celebrating his birthday. Painted brilliant blue and white, it has the characteristic Buick spear down the body. With dark windows and loads of chrome, this car is a real eye-catcher. Its list price in 1957 was $4,053.

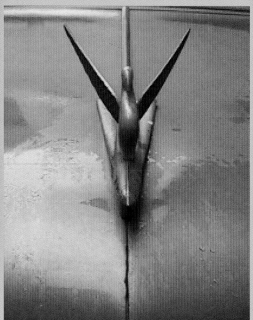

No classic American car was complete without its hood ornament. The emphasis was always on speed and strength. The Dodge ram's head leans forward to break the oncoming wind. The wings of the Cadillac's goddess are pushed back as if in powerful ascent. Buick's streaking bullet broke through a silver ring. A phenomenon peculiar to Cuba is the addition of a winged pelican or swan on the hood as a good luck charm. This mascot traces its lineage back to the Packard of the mid-1930s. Typically affixed on top of the standard ornament with a piece of red string tied around its base, the bird adds a Cuban flourish as it hitches a free ride.

At the northeast corner of Plaza Vieja on Calle Mercaderes was one the most prized of all classic cars, a blue 1959 Cadillac Fleetwood. Its owner, Felix Aldama Perez, was leaning against one of its towering tail fins. It was America's obsession with the Jet Age, aerodynamics and speed in the late 1950s that inspired Dave Holls of General Motors to give birth to the twin fin and double bullet tail lights. With power brakes, power steering, automatic transmission, vanity mirror and two-speed wipers, this car was a steal at $6,233.

A 1956 Buick Roadmaster looking as good as new parked on a quiet street in Old Havana.
The Roadmaster was distinguished from its lesser-priced brethren by the fourth faux vent hole on its front fenders.

Letting sleeping dogs lie. Like flea-bitten mongrels left to their own means, the pitted pride of America's automotive factories lie about the mean streets of Havana starved of gasoline while the bustle of life goes on around them.

It's a fine line between functional service and total abandonment for the automotive relics of another time. But in a land where nothing goes to waste, every scrap will be recycled to keep the running stock of cars on the road.

A modified 1953 Dodge Coronet. Though considered a wolf in sheep's clothing, the '53 Coronet is rumored to have served many high-school Romeos and Juliets as a mild-mannered-looking make-out machine.

A vintage car speeds through a turn as it emerges from a tunnel under Havana's harbor. More Japanese and European cars are appearing on the roads, but with monthly salaries often in single digits, the average Cuban will have to wait a long time for the upgrade.

Seen here outside the main door of the Hotel Nacional is a white 1950 Cadillac Coupe DeVille series 62 hardtop. In Cuba, the elite car in a land of Chevys was the Cadillac. The 1950 Cadillac had a rounded look with baby fins. In fact these fins were not really fins but "tail lamp upsweeps," according to the copywriters. Its heavy doses of chrome represented economic prosperity. The more chrome your car had, the more influence you wielded. It was not uncommon in the pre-revolution days to see sugar barons cruising rural highways in white Cadillacs.

Ramon de la Copa owns a pair 1951 Dodge Kingsways passed down to him through his family. With pale green paintwork and with red bench seats, the two cars are identical in most every way except one: only one is operational. The other is gradually donating vital parts to keep its twin on the road. "This car can tour around Havana, no problem," says Ramon of the operational car. "You see lots of nice cars around, but in reality, when you look underneath…" He trails off and wags his finger disapprovingly. "But mine is all original. Everything original! It's got the original gas tank and it's still working," he says proudly. (Many Cuban cars have plastic "Gerry" cans in their trunks to replace the rusted original gas tanks.)

Looks can be deceiving. While never opulent by northern standards, the interiors of Cuban homes and cars are clean and functional. The exteriors will have to wait for better times.

The 1960 Rambler — prototype for the first Batmobile? The "Good Life" as promised in this 1960 Rambler ad proved to be an illusion for the Cuban car buyer of the time. A revolutionary government was newly in power in Havana, and while they didn't outlaw private car ownership, the U.S. embargo of Cuba, imposed in 1961, made cars and car parts as elusive as the American Dream.

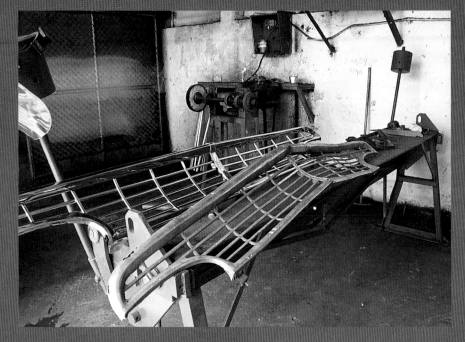

The Chrome Shop

A common ingredient in post-war American cars was the prodigious amounts of chrome used to enhance the look of each model and to distinguish it from all others. If power under the hood was the steak, chrome was the sizzle. Grilles, bumpers, headlights, door handles, window trim, hubcaps and fins — almost everything added to the basic car body was made of chrome or encased in it. Chrome was strong, chrome was shiny, and chrome could be molded into any shape desired.

One thing chrome couldn't do, however, was last forever. Like other parts, chrome components eventually rust out and need to be replaced. At this automotive workshop, they've specialized in making chrome components for American cars since 1978. Based on meticulously created templates or the original worn-out part itself, every new piece is cut, shaped, welded and polished to a high-gloss finish by hand.

And at $130 for a 1955 Ford front grille, it is truly a labor of love.

Habana & Habana Vieja

With over two million people, Havana, or la Habana, is the largest and most ethnically diverse city in the Caribbean. The old town, Habana Vieja, is considered the finest surviving example of a Spanish colonial town in the Americas. Over the years it has fallen into disrepair, with many buildings gutted or torn down, but the situation is turning around. Since 1982, when it was declared a United Nations World Heritage Site, millions of dollars have been spent restoring crumbling buildings to their former grandeur. Cobblestone streets and plazas, linking museums, sidewalk cafés and refurbished hotels are now off limits to cars and trucks. The emerging result of all this work is an urban environment that is more livable for local residents and inviting to the increasing number of tourists who come to visit.

A billboard, roughly translated from Spanish, reads: "Two hundred million children are sleeping on the streets of the world tonight. Not one of them is Cuban." This seems to encapsulate the Cuban dilemma. A strict social doctrine ensures that everyone has a roof over his or her head, but the cost is enormous. Though the United Nations holds Cuba in high regard for its distribution of income, national health care and free and universal education system, average Cubans clearly suffer the economic effects from an over four-decades-long U.S. trade embargo and the

Rumba, the cha-cha-cha and salsa can be heard in even the smallest squares in Habana Vieja, such as here in Plaza de Armas.

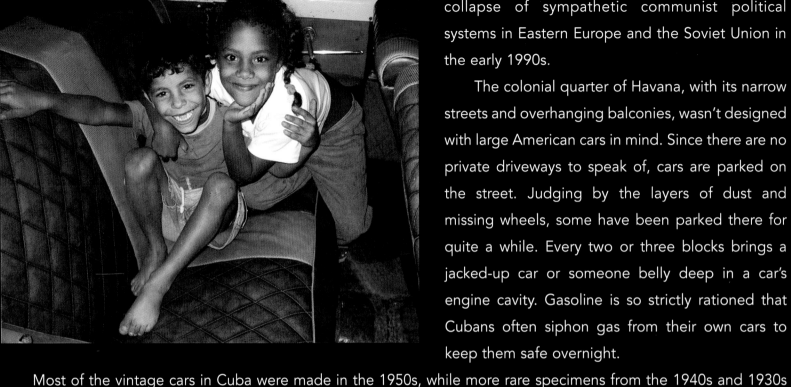

collapse of sympathetic communist political systems in Eastern Europe and the Soviet Union in the early 1990s.

The colonial quarter of Havana, with its narrow streets and overhanging balconies, wasn't designed with large American cars in mind. Since there are no private driveways to speak of, cars are parked on the street. Judging by the layers of dust and missing wheels, some have been parked there for quite a while. Every two or three blocks brings a jacked-up car or someone belly deep in a car's engine cavity. Gasoline is so strictly rationed that Cubans often siphon gas from their own cars to keep them safe overnight.

Most of the vintage cars in Cuba were made in the 1950s, while more rare specimens from the 1940s and 1930s make up the balance. Cuba's surviving American cars are considered a national cultural asset akin to the cable cars of San Francisco. There was a time not long ago when a local Cuban company offered brand-new Ladas in exchange for old American cars. The company then resold them to foreigners for a substantial profit. But the Cuban people recognized the value of these ruggedly preserved cultural icons and put an end to the company's deal-making. Today, cacharro replicas made of ceramics and metal are routinely sold to tourists. The cars are a prominent image found on souvenir T-shirts, and street artists throughout Havana offer paintings of Cuba's colorful Chevys, Fords, Buicks, Cadillacs and DeSotos.

The Plaza de Armas is a beautiful cobblestone square where a horse-and-buggy ride can be had for a couple of dollars.

Hernando de Soto, whose silver-helmeted head once adorned the hood of the DeSoto automobile, was, ironically, Cuba's first governor. It's hard to imagine why he was chosen to represent a line of American cars. As cruel and gold-fevered as any conquistador before him, he pillaged his way through the southern United States, spreading death and disease, until he finally died on the banks of the Mississippi, still searching for a route to China.

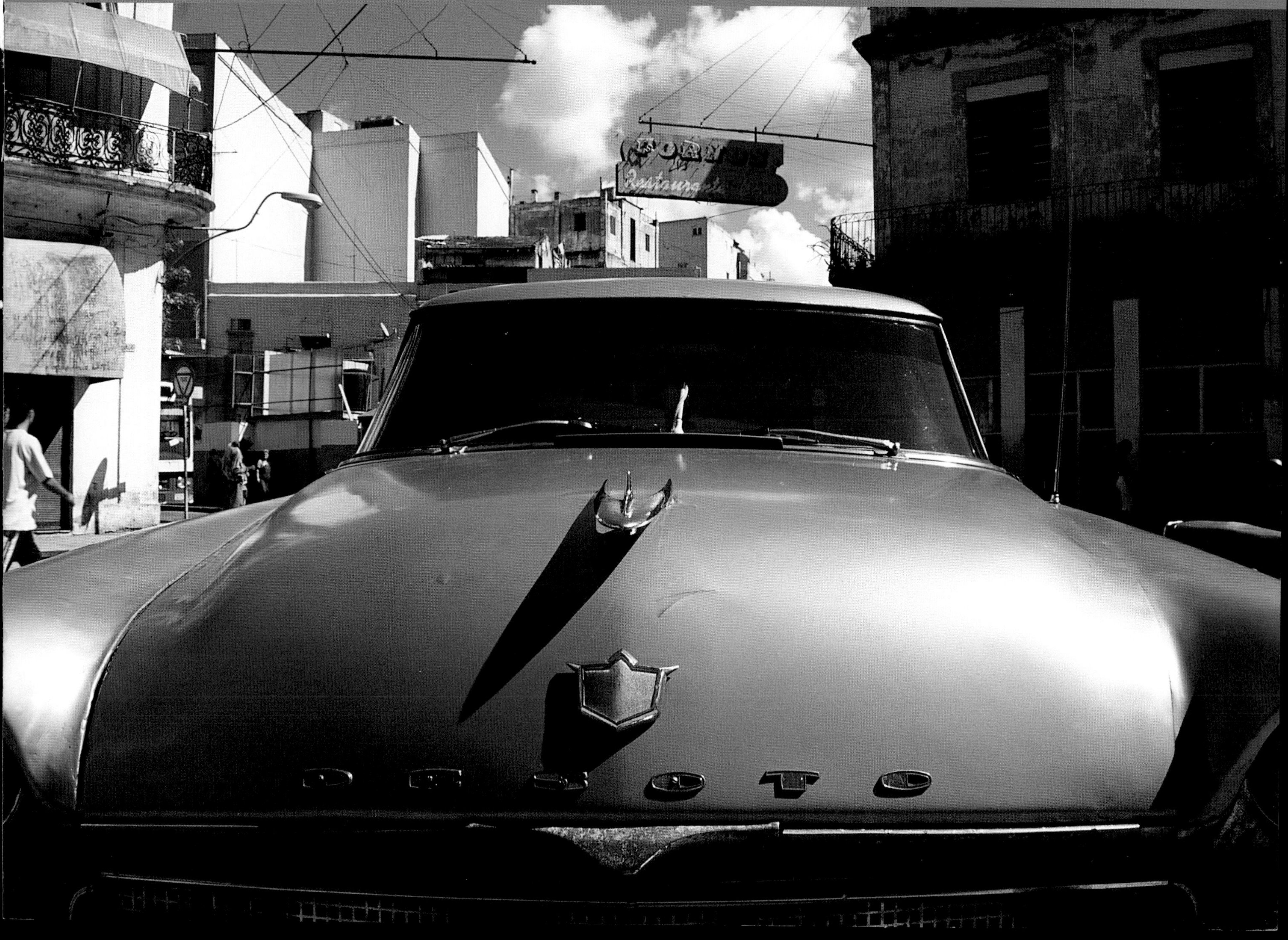

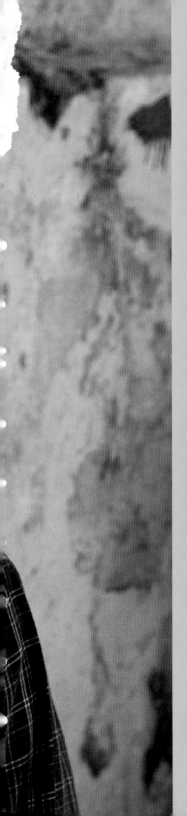

The shoring up and tearing down of ancient buildings goes on at a frenetic pace in Habana Vieja. Care is taken to maintain the distinctive character of the old quarter after some early attempts at modernization became unsightly insults to its architectural past.

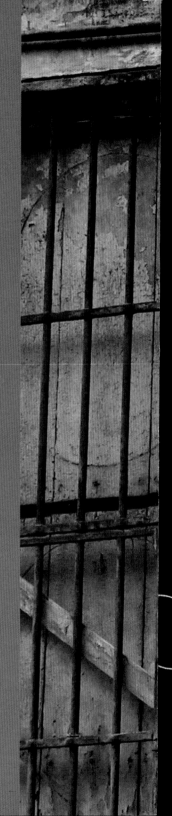

The Blessed Bongo Virgin with Child gives her blessing to even the most worn-out *cacharros*. Now if she could just say a prayer to save the faded facades that provide such an eloquent backdrop for Havana's old cars.

The Automobile Club of Havana

Every once in a while, among all the battered, belching *cacharros* that ply the streets of Havana, you see a vintage car of a different sort, a classic American car in gleaming mint condition. All cars are prized possessions in Cuba, but some cars, the rare ones, have histories that spare them the indignity of growing old and looking their age. Since automobiles remained as private possessions after the Revolution, these cars are typically owned by a single family and lovingly maintained over multiple generations. Having managed to avoid the brutal life of constant travel on rough Cuban roads, they are most likely to be found in private driveways or in front of the better hotels on special occasions, such as a fiesta de quince, a Cuba girl's coming-out party.

Many of the finest cars in Havana are owned by members of a private car club. Once a month, the Automobile Club of Havana gathers at the Hotel Bellocaribe in the Havana suburbs to socialize and talk shop. Throughout the morning, the cars arrive with horns blaring and park in a field beside the hotel. Proud drivers bring their families to swim, barbecue, and of course to show off their meticulously maintained auto heirlooms. Most are 1950s-vintage Chevys, Buicks, Dodges and Fords in near original condition. Their interiors often have been refurbished, and they may sport a modern radio or even a small television. Each car's exterior is polished to a mirror finish. Assembled together, they embody the romance that Cubans have with their American automotive past. Many club members are mechanics, and the club also sponsors philanthropic work, such as restoring an old Russian ambulance to put back into active duty.

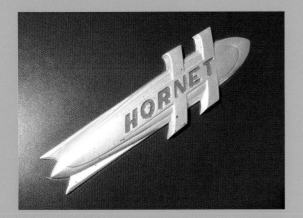

Fabian Villar's
1951 Hudson Hornet

One of the rarest cars in the club, the only working 1951 Hudson Hornet in Cuba is owned by Fabian Villar. With its low, wide, swept-back styling and powerful 308-cubic-inch high-compression six-cylinder L-head engine, the 1951 Hudson Hornet was impressive on the stock car circuit, winning 12 out of 41 NASCAR Grand Nationals that year. Considered by many to be the most unforgettable Hudson of the postwar era, it was prized for its many unique features, including its "step-down" design, which placed the floor on the same level as the chassis, a polished chrome dash with a leather-grain panel, and futuristic rocketship body emblems.

Rolando Pietro Gordillo's 1951 Chevrolet Deluxe

Perhaps Havana's finest example of a 1951 Chevrolet Deluxe is owned by Rolando Pietro Gordillo. According to Gordillo, his car was owned for many years by a little old lady who rarely drove it, preferring to keep it tucked away in a garage for most of its existence. Being an electrician, Gordillo upgraded the car's electrical components. He also had the upholstery restored. Other than that, he insists, his black beauty is completely original, and he has won many prizes to confirm it. His Deluxe is even featured in the logo of the Havana Café, an upscale disco in the center of town. This car was Chevrolet's top seller in 1951. A total of 855,293 Styleline Deluxe models were produced out of a total 1951 Chevrolet production run of 1,250,803 cars. The base price for this model was about $1,600.

Armando Pascual Goñzales's
1955 Chevrolet

Engine mechanic Armando Pascual Goñzales has not one but two vintage American cars, a 1955 Chevrolet parked in the driveway and a 1948 Studebaker Commander that is being worked on in the garage. With its new "small block" V-8 engine, the 180-horsepower, overdrive-equipped 1955 Chevrolet could reach a top speed of about 105 miles per hour. It had hooded headlights and an elaborate forward-canted grille, a style that Chevrolet's literature called "Motoramic." This 1955 model proved to be one of the most popular Chevrolets ever made.

Armando Pascual Goñzales's
1948 Studebaker Commander
The 1948 Studebaker Commander has
that distinct Studebaker rear end but not
the well-known chrome-plated bullet nose,
which debuted in 1950.

Delis Ramon Aguilera Peña's
1957 4-door Pontiac Chieftain

On a quiet, leafy suburban street, away from the heat and fumes of Old Havana, sits an immaculate 1957 4-door Pontiac Chieftain. This was a stylish year for many car lines, and Pontiac introduced its "Starflight" look, with missile-shaped side trim and extended rear fenders with V-shaped tips. This particular car was made by General Motors of Canada and is owned by Señor Delis Ramon Aguilera Peña, a retired veterinarian. "Of course it's better to have the original motor and parts. She's got Russian pistons. She's not the most economical of cars. I get only eight or nine kilometers per liter [about 20 miles per gallon]," says Aguilera Peña.

Noel Trujillo Trujillo's
1952 Ford truck

Though Noel Trujillo's '52 Ford truck, with its loads of chrome and cherry-red paint, looks like a super-sized confection in a candy store, he still works it as part of his business. Its refinements and its sturdiness speak to his skills as an auto customizer and mechanic.

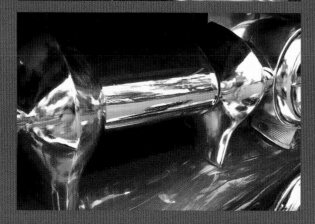

Noel Trujillo Trujillo's
1957 Mercury Monterey

Noel Trujillo Trujillo and his son are engine mechanics on the outskirts of Havana. Together, they have refurbished two beauties, a sleek white 1957 Mercury Monterey and an enhanced red 1952 Ford truck. Mercurys had previously been thought of as "Fords with more chrome," but in 1957 Mercury promoted its own "Dream-Car" design: "Styled to influence the shape of cars for years to come." Check out the headlights. Its base price was around $2,700, and it featured a 312-cubic-inch 255-horsepower V-8 and a push-button Merc-O-Matic transmission.

Julio Palmero Pedriane's
1957 Chevy Bel Air

Julio Palmero Pedriane flashed a broad smile as he polished his 1957 Chevy Bel Air affectionately. He knows it's a classic beauty. The '57 Chevy is one of the most sought-after models among car collectors. With its oval grille and bomb-shaped bumpers, it epitomizes the style of the time. The top-of-the-line Bel Air model had extra chrome molding and features such as the three gold chevrons on each front fender. This was also the year that Chevrolet became a serious performance entry with its new 283-cubic-inch V-8 engine that produced one horsepower per cubic inch.

Justo Pastor Lima Rizo's
1957 Ford Custom

The key to Justo Pastor Lima Rizo's 1957 green-and-turquoise Ford Custom was as worn as the car itself. This car

has been well driven but has withstood the test of time. The '57 Fords were completely restyled. They were longer, lower and wider than 1956 models and sported the latest automotive design craze, tailfins — or "high-canted fenders," as Ford referred to them.

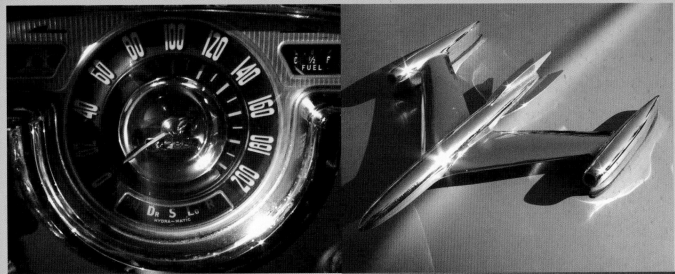

Adrian Garcia Alonzo's
1954 Oldsmobile Super 88

With chrome rocket emblems on its body and Saturn imbedded in its steering wheel, Adrian Garcia Alonzo's "Futuramic"-styled 1954 Oldsmobile Super 88 predates Sputnik and the space race. Oldsmobile ads described their car as "long and low-level, lithe and so lovely! With a sports-car flair in the sweep-cut of its door and fender lines...the dramatic arch of its panoramic windshield...This Super '88' is styled for the open road." And the driver should be advised that the "Rocket" engine "responds instantly to your every wish!"

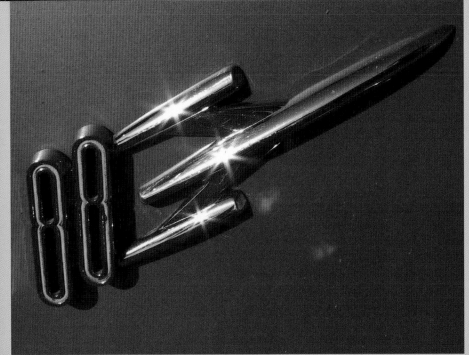

Miguel Cordero Capote's
1953 Ford Customline

Even with UV-tinted windows and a metallic brown paint job, this 1953 Ford Customline was not the most attractive vehicle we'd seen. But it was the pride of its owner, Miguel Cordero Capote and better off than the hulk of metal on blocks across the street. Ford Motor Company celebrated its fiftieth anniversary in 1953. Three quarters of a million Customlines were produced that year, at a base sticker price of about $1,800, and powered by either six cylinders or the legendary flathead V-8 with overdrive.

Luis Barros Brea's
1954 Dodge Kingsway

What a beautiful car — Luis Barros Brea's sky-blue four-door 1954 Dodge Kingsway. There seems to be multiple styles for the logo, perhaps because of the Kingsway's "for export" category. The name Kingsway was never used in the United States, where these cars were called the Meadowbrook, or the Coronet if they sported extra trim. Chrysler had a habit of re-branding Plymouths as Dodges for the export market. In the 1950s every Plymouth body design was also offered as either a Dodge or a DeSoto. For example, the 1959 Plymouth Savoy model was sold as a Dodge Kingsway for overseas export, as a Dodge Regent for the Canadian market, and as a DeSoto Diplomat. By any name, it's a great ride.

Jorge Luis M. Hernandez's
1960 Oldsmobile Dynamic 88

With its forward-tilted struts and wraparound window, Jorge Luis M. Hernandez's 1960 Oldsmobile Dynamic 88 looks like it once starred on the animated television series *The Jetsons*. American cars from 1960 are not common in Cuba. The Revolution succeeded in '59 and the embargo was imposed in 1961. Señor Hernandez explains that this car once belonged to a foreign *professora*, a woman teacher who didn't stay on in revolutionary Cuba. An Oldsmobile 98 convertible was the official pace car at the 1960 Indianapolis 500.

The Mechanic Shop

Eliecer Gomez is a mechanic with a mission: to restore his 1951 Buick Special to its original condition. Sitting on blocks in the courtyard of his workshop, the buck-toothed Buick grille seems to smile at all the attention it receives. But parts are hard to come by, and it will be a while before his favorite car is back on the road. Meanwhile, there is work to be done on an old ambulance that is being rehabilitated by the car club members as a goodwill project.

Lazaro Perdano Peñalver's
1949 Buick Super Eight

The exterior of Lazaro Perdano Peñalver's 1949 Buick Super Eight behemoth was basic black and chrome, but inside, in keeping with the Cuban taste for bold colors, he had painted the molded metal dashboard brilliant magenta. This was the year that Buick added its three distinctive chrome "ventiports" to the front fenders. A cigar lighter was among the standard features — not just on models exported to Cuba.

Jorge Diaz Regalado's 1956 Pontiac

Jorge Diaz Regalado lives in a quiet village on the outskirts of Havana. His 1956 Pontiac is anything but quiet, however. He keeps the engine souped up and growling. In its day, this four-door sedan could go from 0 to 60 in just 11.4 seconds. With its chrome alloy wheels and the Pontiac name stretching across its windshield, Jorge's pride and joy presents the look of a stock car ready to race. This was the last year that Pontiacs sported broad chrome bands across their hoods, a feature that had defined the Pontiac look in the early '50s.

Francisco Sarmiento Fazio's
1954 Chevrolet Bel Air

Given the heat of high noon in Havana, it's surprising that you don't find more vintage convertibles on the roads. This bright red 1954 Chevrolet Bel Air convertible is owned by Francisco Sarmiento Fazio. He enjoys taking it out for a spin, but replacing parts is a big problem. He can't import them from the United States because of the decades-long embargo. He's heard there's an owner of a similar model up in Canada, and he'd like to contact her to see if she can help him locate parts. The 1954 Bel Airs were powered by either Synchromesh or Powerglide inline sixes. The Powerglide option, with new high-lift camshafts, cost $178. Power brakes were $38, power front windows $86, and power steering $135.

Photographer Alberto Korda and Stock Car Champion Elias Regalado

These black-and-white photographs of Elias Regalado were taken by Cuban photographer Alberto Díaz Gutiérrez (Korda), 1928-2001. Born in Havana, the son of a railway worker, the young Alberto Korda took up photography "to meet women." He established himself as a successful fashion photographer and changed his surname from Díaz Gutiérrez to Korda because "it sounded like Kodak."

He spent ten years as Fidel Castro's official photographer and is responsible for photographs of the Cuban leader in off-duty moments with Ernest Hemingway and Jean-Paul Sartre.

It was while on an assignment for *Revolución* in 1960 that Korda took the famous photo of Che. He was panning his camera when Che's face jumped into his viewfinder. The look in Che's eyes startled Korda so much that he instinctively lurched backwards and snapped the shot. Che was later killed in Bolivia, becoming an instant martyr. When Castro addressed a memorial rally in Havana's Plaza de la Revolución, Korda's photo was used as a mural on the building facing the podium. It remains one of Cuba's most prominent landmarks and one of the world's best-known images.

In the 1950s Elias Regalado worked for Partagas, one of the large Cuban tobacco companies. As an employee, he drove trucks loaded with cigarettes between Havana and Santiago de Cuba, more than 500 miles to the east. But on his own time, Regalado and his friends developed their passion for racing stock cars.

When Buick chose Regalado to be part of their racing team, it was a dream come true. Behind the wheel of the latest Buicks, with their weight reduced and their engines rigged to run on kerosene, Regalado soon proved himself a *campeon*.

In 1955 he won his big race, a stock car rally from Sagua to Havana, in a record time of just under two hours, at an average speed of 94.5 miles per hour. With a champion's trophy and a pocket full of winnings, truck-driver Elias Regalado became the toast of Havana.

Elias Regalado, retired racing champion.

Beyond Havana

Beyond Havana and all its contradictions, away from the beaches and their opulent resorts, another Cuba, poor and pastoral, awaits the intrepid traveler. Rich in history, bio-diversity and traditional ways, rural Cuba has the balm to soothe a world–weary soul. Roads are generally good and traffic is light, though signage is quite poor. Hotels are few but the B & B concept, called *Casa Particular*, has spread to every town and village. At $15 to $20 a night, it's a wonderful way to interact with the locals and share their simple hospitality.

The view from the lookout at Los Jazmines Hotel. The Val de Vigñales is a stunningly luxuriant landscape of limestone hills, palm trees and tobacco plantations.

There are so few buses in Cuba that hitchhiking is often the only way to get from place to place. Soldiers, farmers, children and the elderly can be seen on the edge of every town and village, waiting for a free ride.

The "overpass to nowhere" at least provides shade for the people who gather beneath it to hitch a ride down the highway. The National Highway, built with Soviet help, runs the length of the country but is under-utilized due to the shortage of cars, trucks and buses and the relatively high cost of gasoline.

The most popular working man's car, Chevrolets are still everywhere in sight, along with aging Fords and Plymouths.
They seem too mechanical and noisy for this pastoral setting where time almost stands still.

With its limestone hillocks and rich red earth, the valley of Viñales is one of the most picturesque areas in Cuba. Most farmers still work
their fields with oxen and plow and live in thatch-roofed cottages called *bohios*. This part of Cuba is a prime tobacco-growing area and its
farmers were once wealthy enough to afford new cars.

"Piñar! Piñar!" hollers the *botero* driver like a town crier. He is announcing his departure for Piñar del Rio, but only one passenger, a *campesino* in his best blue shirt and sombrero, is waiting by the car. Time is flexible in this part of the world, and this prospective passenger knows he might wait all afternoon until the *botero* is full enough to make the journey.

A customized 1955 Chevrolet parked by the road from Viñales to Piñar del Rio. This car has a polished finish unusual for the countryside. Refitted with a Hyundai engine, it is owned and maintained by Orlando Loza, a pastor at the Free Baptist Church in Piñar.

Artemisa, named after Artemis, the Greek god of fertility, is an attractive agricultural center of 160,000 with a strong cultural tradition and several museums. The large number of mid-1950s cars found here is a sign of its former prosperity.

Schoolchildren in Artemisa's Casa de la Cultura rehearse for an upcoming festival.

The streets of Matanzas are alive with the hustle and bustle of daily life. Cubans live on the streets – it is an extension of their living rooms. Sex, music and dancing, they like to say, are their greatest pleasures, as none are rationed and all are free.

In Matanzas, the driver of many an iron-lunged *cacharro* can put his foot to the gas pedal and still not go much faster than the two-wheel pedal power.

At the Finca Tres Palmas near Cienfuegos farm owner Abelardo Garcia Sanabria just happened to have in his barn a blue-and-beige Ford Edsel Ranger, which he graciously consented to bring out into the light of day. The 1958 Edsel Ranger was the cheapest Edsel at $2,519. It came with "Teletouch" push-button automatic transmission controls in the steering wheel. Doomed from the minute it was unveiled, the Edsel made the marketing slogan "Here to Stay" a cruel joke for Ford.

In small towns throughout the country, women gather on stoops at the end of the day to discuss their families or to gossip, or perhaps to complain about the shortage of food or the long line-ups. Yet, despite their many hardships, Cubans *joie de vivre* remains intact, and when one asks a Cuban, "How are you?" the answer is often "En la lucha!" ("Struggling!"), usually said with a smile.

Jose D'Modiedo and his son get ready for the Sunday family drive in their green 1948 Plymouth two-door sedan. This particular model had an unusual glass hood ornament that lit up at night.

Single-story ochre-colored houses with peeling plaster and crumbling façades are a common sight in Trinidad de Cuba. Residents take frequent siestas in front of the ornate grilled windows to pass the hot days.

With the historic Iglesia de la Santisima Trinidad towering high above the town behind her,
five-year-old Margelis sits on the hood of her father's red-and-white 1952 Chevrolet Styleline Deluxe.

Trinidad de Cuba has changed little over the 500 years since its founding. The Plaza Mayor, with its old cathedral and colonial palaces basking in a golden morning light, is off limits to vehicles, making it a peaceful place to contemplate the town's rich history.

1952 Chevy 210

Rentar una Fantasia

Rentar una Fantasia! The words jumped off the glossy color brochure, tempting and teasing us. Dazzling white Cadillac convertibles with sumptuous red interiors, sleek Chevy Impalas and two-toned Buicks shimmered before my eyes. The muscle cars of the 1950s, with their mountains of chrome, fabulous fins and monster engines, were all available — for a price!

Large rental operations such as Caribe and Panacar make their vintage cars available to tourists, and each wide-bodied beauty has been maintained with as much original detail as possible. What better way to discover the land of cigars, Castro and Che than from the inside a classic 1957 Chevy. These metallic "Yank Tanks" ply the calles and barrios of Havana spewing forth memorable clouds of exhaust. Anyone can visit Havana, but to truly experience it, get behind the wheel of one of these chariots of chrome. Or better yet, settle into the vast backseat of a '50s Chevy and let yourself be chauffeured. Prices run about $15 US dollars per hour or $90 per day with gas. Rental cars are easily identified by their blue license plates. Their drivers-for-hire often moonlight as mechanics and tour guides and generally have a good command of English. Most drivers are well briefed on the origins of each car, and a full description and history of the particular model is usually provided at the onset of the excursion.

Rentar una fantasia is operated by Grancar, which is owned by Panautos Rent a Car. They maintain a fleet of approximately 39 classic American cars from the

1930s through the '50s. Grancar scours the country in search of classic cars whose owners are willing to part with their most prized possession for $2,000 to $4,000 US dollars. It's often a difficult decision. These *cacharros* are loved and pampered by their owners. They are family heirlooms that have been handed down through two or three generations of a single family, witnesses to courtships, marriages, births and deaths.

Since private ownership of cars is unofficially frowned upon in Cuba, few citizens receive government permission to purchase new cars, and then there is the high cost of gas — roughly equivalent to two months average salary to "fill 'er up." This fact often makes the decision to sell a *cacharro* more appealing.

Once Grancar purchases a car, it is repaired and restored to its original condition, or as much as possible given the shortage of parts. Once a new coat of paint is applied, the cars are put to work on the streets, where they are hired by filmmakers, local wedding planners or tourists with a taste for nostalgia.

Such rental fantasy cars are often found parked in strategic locations throughout Havana to entice gringos who can afford to fantasize. The Melia Cohiba, Inglaterra, Hotel Habana Libre, the Riviera and the Nacional all have cars on standby for a tailpipe-popping blast from the past.

A 1952 Chevy Deluxe parked at the Capitolio in Havana is passed by a "Bicitaxi," the Cuban equivalent of a rickshaw, a two-seated chair welded onto a bicycle frame. Not too comfortable, but the view is great!

Running into the Plaza de la Catedral is Empedrado Street, home to the famous watering hole Bodeguita del Medio. It was *the* celebrity hangout in its day. Nat King Cole, Brigitte Bardot, Carmen Miranda and Ernest Hemingway all came to have their mojitoes here and supposedly left their names in the graffiti scribbled on its walls. If you had lived here during the late '50s, you might have seen Hemingway drive the narrow Empedrado in his huge 1955 Chrysler New Yorker Deluxe.

Outside the Bodeguita, Francisco Gomez, wife Aleida Rosabal Sanchez and their children pose in front of their olive-green 1950 Chevrolet Styleline Special. This car is in mint condition. The steering wheel and seats are in matching brown quilted imitation leather, and the factory radio and clock are still in working order.

Elson Caballero leans against his copper-colored Chevrolet 210, with its twin rocket-shaped wind splits. Behind him are the Plaza de *Revolución* and the towering silhouette of Che Guevara on the façade of the Ministry of the Interior. Che was a man of the people and refused to drive anything flashier than a Chevy Impala. His cohorts in the government ministries, however, preferred the Cadillacs that became available when businesses and property were nationalized after the Revolution.

Adelaida Borges fans herself beside her yellow-and-white 1953 Chevy Bel Air, parked under the neon lights of the famous Floridita. The Floridita claims to serve the best daiquiri in town. Ernest Hemingway was known to be a regular. Adelaida is wearing enough jewelry on her fingers, wrists, neck, ears and ankles to make a even a flashy '59 Cadillac envious.

No trip to Cuba would be complete without a cruise through the countryside and along the beaches of this delightful country. To this end, Rentar una Fantasia delivered a brown-and-beige 1956 Buick Special for the final two days of our stay. A huge showboat of a car, the Special was perfect for our trip to Trinidad de Cuba. On the way, we passed through St. Rosa del Rosario, where a group of uniformed schoolchildren from the Escuela Bartalome Maso gave us a warm Cuban reception.

Bienvenidos — classic car lovers are truly welcome in Cuba.